NO AR

W9-DJG-604

Everything You Need To Know About

YOUR
LEGAL
RIGHTS

Every individual has certain rights that can never be taken away.

• THE NEED TO KNOW LIBRARY •

Everything You Need To Know About

YOUR LEGAL RIGHTS

Kenneth Fox, Ph.D.

THE ROSEN PUBLISHING GROUP, INC.
NEW YORK

Published in 1992, 1995, 1999 by The Rosen Publishing Group, Inc.
29 East 21st Street, New York, NY 10010

Revised Edition 1999

Library of Congress Cataloging-in-Publication Data

Fox, Kenneth.
 Everything you need to know about your legal rights / Kenneth Fox.
 (The Need to know library)
 Includes bibliographical references and index.
 Summary: Briefly discusses the legal rights of individuals, emphasizing real-life situations in which teenagers may find themselves.
 ISBN 0-8239-2872-1
 1. Minors—United States—Juvenile literature. 2. Civil rights—United States—Juvenile literature. [1. Law. 2. Children's rights. 3. Civil rights.] I. Title. II. Title: Your legal rights. III. Series.
 KF479.Z9F697   1992
 342.73'085—dc20
 [347.30285]
                                                              91-13340
                                                                  CIP
                                                                   AC

Manufactured in the United States of America.

Contents

Introduction

Today the Constitution of the United States guarantees all its citizens certain basic *rights*. But the Constitution didn't always protect the rights of everyone. When it was first created, many thought the Constitution didn't give enough protection to people.

Since its creation, the Constitution has been amended, or changed, many times. The *Bill of Rights* (the first ten amendments) was added to assure certain individual rights to the people, including freedom of speech, freedom of religion, the right to privacy, the right to bear arms, and the right to a fair trial.

Many other amendments have also been added over the years. For example, after the Civil War the 13th Amendment abolished slavery. In 1920, another amendment, the 19th, gave women the right to vote.

It may surprise you to learn that these basic rights

Freedom of the press allows people to publish their opinions openly, without control by the government.

have not always been extended to minors (anyone under the age of eighteen). At one time, young people did not have the right to a fair trial. A young person accused of a crime might be put in a juvenile hall for years whether or not he or she was guilty. In fact, it has only been in the last twenty-five years that legal rights for young people have been expanded.

Freedom of speech, for example, was not extended to minors in school until 1969. When students at an Iowa high school were suspended for wearing black armbands to school in protest of the Vietnam War, they took the school to court and won. The decision in *Tinker* v. *Des Moines* stated that students' rights to freedom of speech do not disappear once they enter the school grounds. This victory was just the beginning of the debate surrounding teens' legal rights.

Times have changed and continue to change. Teens now have the right to due process, or a fair trial, in juvenile court. They now have privacy rights in matters of birth control and abortion. Young people everywhere are becoming more and more involved in their legal rights. Organizations such as the American Civil Liberties Union (ACLU) are helping teens understand how to defend their rights, because sometimes teen rights are violated even though laws exist to protect them. Being aware of your rights will help you make sure they are enforced.

As violence in schools rises and parents and teachers become concerned over teen drug use, more and more restrictions are being placed on teens. Some of these restrictions include strict curfews; bans on over-the-counter drugs in schools, such as aspirin and ibuprofen; bans on pagers; bans on selling spray paint (because of graffiti); and mandatory drug testing at school dances.

Parents, lawmakers, and teachers may support these restrictions. Many laws are put in place for your protection. You may agree that these laws are good and keep you safe. Or you may believe that your rights are being violated and that certain restrictions go too far.

Understanding your legal rights can be complicated. That's because the laws themselves are complicated. It is not always clear how and to whom a law should be applied. It is up to the courts to decide how to apply a law, and sometimes this can vary from state to state.

For example, in some states a person under eighteen accused of murder cannot be tried as an adult. In other states, the age is sixteen and in some it is fourteen. Still others have no age limit at all. This means that, in some states, a twelve-year-old charged with murder can be tried as an adult.

This book explains what your rights are, how you can fight a law you believe is unfair, and what to expect if you do decide to fight. You'll find answers for questions about laws at school, at home, on the job, and at the mall.

If you've ever wondered whether your school can search your locker for no reason, whether you can still go to school if you're pregnant, or whether your parents can secretly use a home drug test on you, this book is for you. Even if you have never had an issue with your legal rights, it's very likely that you will do so at some point in your life. Knowing your rights before something happens will give you the power to know what your options are and even to make a change in the system.

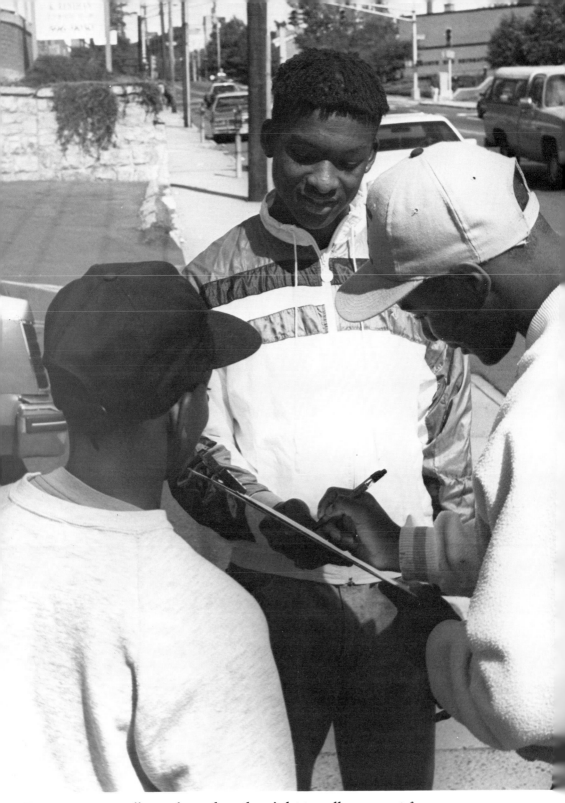

Everyone, regardless of age, has the right to rally support for a particular cause.

Chapter 1

Young People's Rights: Protection and Limits

*J*anine Givens and her friend Lee Palmer are 11
years old. They live in Andover, Massachusetts.
When they had a report to write for school, they went
to the public library.

They found only a few useful books in the
children's section, so they went to the adult section.
The librarian told them they had to be 12 to be
allowed in the adult section. She made them go back
to the children's section.

Janine's mother became upset when she heard
what had happened. She tried to find out whether the
girls would be allowed in the adult section if they had
their parents' permission.

She found out that the library rule applied to all
children under 12, whether or not they had their
parents' permission. The purpose of the rule was to
make sure adults were not disturbed.

Asserting Your Rights

Janine and Lee decided the library rules were keeping them from exercising an important right: the right to read. They decided to do something to get the library to change its rules.

They circulated a petition asking the library to change the rule. The petition was signed by 150 children. Local newspapers learned of the petition and printed stories about it. A large color photo of Janine and Lee holding the petition appeared in the Sunday paper.

Janine's mother and other parents said that they supported the petition also. They did not think the library had a good reason for its rule. They recognized that there were reasons for limiting young people's rights. But they did not think the library should limit their children's right to read.

Reasons for Limits on Your Rights

Everyone enjoys the same rights. Adults may exercise their rights fully. As a young person you possess the same rights, but your use of those rights can be limited for three important reasons.

• Protection

The first reason is the need for protection. Your parents have a legal responsibility to protect and care for you. In order to do this, they may limit your rights.

Your local government can also limit your rights to protect you. For example, some towns have curfews requiring young people under age 16 or 14 to be off the streets after 10:00 p.m. These curfews are meant to protect you from danger or prevent you from getting into trouble.

Some parents make many rules and punish their children for breaking these rules. They believe rules are an important way to protect their children from harm. If your parents are very strict, you may think you have no rights at all. But this is not true. Your parents can protect you by limiting your rights, but they cannot take your rights away completely.

• **Lack of Maturity**

The second reason for limiting young people's rights is their lack of maturity. Young people's powers of reasoning are not fully developed. They are often not able to separate what is good for them from what is harmful.

The PG-13 restriction on many movies states that children under 13 cannot see the movie unless accompanied by a parent or guardian. This restriction shows how limits are lifted as young people become more mature. If you are 13 or older, you are considered mature enough to see PG-13 movies without parental supervision.

Restrictions on young people's right to vote are also based on their lack of mature judgment. You cannot vote until you become 18. Until 1971, the voting age was 21. It was reduced to 18 because most people had come to believe that 18-year-olds were mature enough to vote responsibly.

• Conflict with Your Parents' Rights

The third limitation on young people's rights arises from conflict with the rights of their parents. One of the most important rights of parents is the right to decide how their children will be educated. Another is the right to determine their children's religion.

If your parents think that certain books will interfere with the way they want you to grow up, they have the right to prevent you from reading those books. In some towns, the public library keeps young people from borrowing certain books when their parents request such restriction.

You *Can* Fight City Hall

While your rights can be limited, you should never feel that your rights can be taken away.

"You can't fight city hall," people often say. They are wrong. We have the rights we have today because people throughout our history have stood up against rules and laws they believed were wrong. They fought city hall and won.

Andover's library officials are considering whether the policy should be changed. Janine and Lee are waiting to see if their petition has succeeded. If you lived in Andover, would you sign Janine and Lee's petition? Are children restricted from the adult section of the library in your community?

Chapter 2

Parental Abuse and Other Rights Violations

Many of your rights are limited by your parents. According to law, they have the right to tell you where to live, how to live, how to dress, what religion to practice, even how to choose your friends. In a way, your family is like an absolute monarchy in which your parents are king and queen and you are their subject. However, in most families, parents listen to their children before they make rules, so that the rules are more fair.

Your parents have many responsibilities that go along with their rights over you. They must never do anything that can harm you. That means that they must make sure you get a good education, have a place to live, eat well, and stay healthy physically. It also means trying to ensure that you are happy and that you have the freedom to develop and learn about life. They may not *abuse* you mentally or physically.

Unfortunately, some parents forget or overlook these responsibilities. Thousands of children are abused in the United States when their parents do not accept these responsibilities. Children are beaten, verbally abused, neglected, even sexually abused.

If your parents do not fulfill their responsibilities, they are committing a crime. They can be arrested and jailed. If they still do not treat you properly, the courts may take you away from them. Another family would then be selected to take care of you.

Child Abuse

Amy's parents divorced when she was eight. Five years later, her mother remarried. At first, Amy was happy for her mom, but soon after the wedding things began to change.

Amy started fighting more and more with her stepfather. She was starting high school in the fall, and she was spending more time out at night with her friends. Since she was getting older, Amy thought that she deserved more freedom. But Amy's stepfather didn't agree. He was very strict with her, and Amy's mother let him make the rules.

One night, Amy asked permission to go to a party. Her stepfather refused. In the heat of anger, Amy told her stepfather she hated him and wished he wasn't a part of her family. He slapped her and shoved her against the wall. Shocked and stunned, she spent the rest of the night in her room.

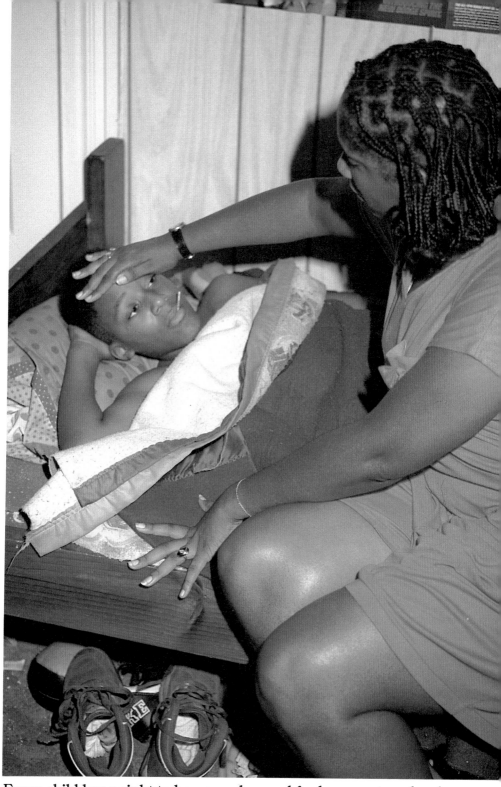

Every child has a right to be properly cared for by parents or legal guardians.

The next morning, her mom promised it would never happen again. But it did. Amy's stepfather physically abused her anytime she disagreed with him.

Amy's best friend, Sarah, noticed Amy's bruises. When she asked about them, Amy began to cry. Amy said she was so scared she didn't know what to do. Together, they went to Sarah's mom, who called the local child protective agency.

Two days later, the child protective agency conducted an investigation. A team of social workers came to Amy's house unannounced. They interviewed Amy, her mother, and her stepfather.

The child protective agency believed Amy was in danger and filed a petition in family court to take Amy out of her home. Amy stayed with Sarah's family, and the court ordered Amy's mom and stepfather to get counseling to deal with their problems.

A month later, Amy moved back into her home. Her stepfather has stopped physically abusing her, and their relationship is improving. To make sure she is safe, a social worker makes regular visits to the house and provides counseling for Amy's family.

Child Neglect

Your parents are responsible for supporting you and taking care of your physical needs. If they do not care for you well enough, they are violating your rights. This is called *neglect*. Neglect is not always intentional. Your parents may be trying their best.

Sometimes children suffer neglect because their parents are away from home a great deal. Sometimes they cannot afford to buy food or clothing because all the money goes to pay the rent.

Parents are sometimes unaware of programs that can help them. *Medicaid* can help with medical costs, and *food stamps* can help with groceries. Some programs help pay the rent or the cost of heating in the winter.

If You Are Abused or Neglected

If your parent hits you, sexually molests you, or neglects you (failing to take care of you and leaving you to fend for yourself), you have the right to take action to protect yourself.

When you have a big problem, you probably first turn to your parents for help. But whom do you turn to when your parents are the problem?

Talk with someone you trust. Speak with a teacher or a counselor at school, a religious leader, a coach, or the sponsor of a school club whom you feel comfortable approaching. If this makes you uncomfortable, call one of the hotlines listed on page 61.

The most important thing to remember is that what is happening to you is not your fault. *No one ever deserves to be abused or neglected.* You have the right to be safe.

Divorce is the legal separation of two married people. Often, one of the parents is given custody of the children.

Chapter 3

Separation and Divorce

Separation and divorce are very traumatic events both for parents and their children. On top of the stress the situations create, all the laws that go along with them can be very confusing. It's hard to understand how a decision of your parents can affect your rights so drastically.

When married people *separate,* they agree to live in separate places. This allows them to decide whether they will get back together or choose to divorce. A *divorce* is when two people legally end their marriage. They must go to court to seek the right to divorce.

When parents separate or divorce, they or a judge must decide which parent will have custody of you. *Custody* means whom you live with, who is responsible for you, and who will make major decisions about your life. Sometimes parents are given *joint custody,* which means you live with both parents at different times, and they share responsibility. Sometimes one parent has custody, and the other has *visitation rights*. This means that the parent you live with must permit your other parent to see you. Usually the divorce or separation agreement decides how often you see your noncustodial parent.

Usually parents themselves decide who has custody. But sometimes neither parent is willing to give up custody of the child. They both want to live with their child. In this case, a judge makes the decision. The judge may ask you what you would like, or he or she may decide without asking you.

Sometimes it can be hard on you not being allowed to decide who you will live with. Many children don't have a chance to tell a judge what they want.

The Child's Best Interests

Tim knew he wanted to live with his dad after the divorce. His mom was nice and all, but his dad was great. They would go fishing together, watch ball games. Life with Dad would be great. And Mom was so much stricter. If Tim had to live with her, he knew he wouldn't have as much freedom.

When Tim's parents told him that they had decided he was to live with his mom, he was really upset. They hadn't even asked him what he wanted. Why couldn't he live with his dad? Didn't his dad love him?

His parents tried to explain to Tim that his father was out of town so often on business that it would be more stable for him to live with his mother. But Tim was furious that a decision about his life had been made for him without even asking him what he thought.

It may seem unfair that you don't get to choose where and with whom you live. But that's the law. And there is a good reason for the law. Tim might have preferred living with his father, but his father was away from home a lot. Tim would have ended up spending most of his time alone or with baby-sitters. His parents made the decision that they thought would be best for him.

If you think your parents made the wrong decision about custody, talk to them. Tell them how you feel, and listen to what they have to say. Your parents would not make such an important decision about you without thinking about it first. And remember, whatever you think, they have the right to decide where you live.

Our compulsory education laws mean that children from age 6 to 16 must go to school and must have the choice of a free education.

Chapter 4

Do I Have to Go to School?

"I *hate school," Ramone complained as his mother shook him awake. "Why do I have to go to school? We never learn anything. All our teacher ever says is 'Be quiet! Get back in your seat!'"*

Compulsory Education

Going to school is one of your legal rights. The constitution of your state provides that you have the right to a free education. These laws are called the *compulsory education laws.* They provide that all children from age 6 to age 16 must receive an education.

Compulsory education laws were passed around 100 years ago for two reasons. The first reason was to prevent parents from forcing their children to go to work. Before, parents had the right to send their children to work instead of to school. These laws gave parents the responsibility of making sure that their children received an education.

25

The second reason for these laws was to require cities and towns to build schools and hire the necessary teachers. In the past, communities often failed to raise the money needed to build new schools.

Public Schools, Parochial Schools, and Private Schools

Your city or town is required to make sure there is room for you in the public school system. But you do not have to go to a public school. Many children attend parochial schools run by churches and religious groups. Other children attend private schools with no religious connections. Most of the money to run these schools comes from parents of children who attend them. Cities and towns usually don't pay for the education of children attending parochial or private schools.

Your Rights at School

Kalli was the opinion column editor at the school newspaper. She wrote a column criticizing the principal for cutting money from drama and music programs, but not sports teams. When the paper came out, the principal suspended Kalli and recalled the papers.

Being a journalist helped Kalli fight for her rights. She knew that under certain circumstances the school could censor the newspaper. But she also knew the principal was violating her First Amendment rights. Kalli decided to appeal the principal's decision. The school board conducted a hearing and found in Kalli's favor.

Unlike most printed material, your school newspaper can be censored.

The U.S. Supreme Court decision *Hazelwood School District* v. *Kuhlmeier* gives a school the right to censor a student newspaper. But studying First Amendment law helped Kalli. She knew that her school newspaper had a history of publishing student opinion. And she knew the *Hazelwood* decision didn't apply to a student publication that had a specific space for student expression. It wasn't easy to address the school board, but knowing her rights helped her win her case.

Child labor laws say that a person must be at least 16 years old in order to work legally.

Chapter 5

What If I Want to Work?

*P*erry is 13, but he is very tall for his age. He got a job at a gas station pumping gas from 3 in the afternoon until 11 at night. The station wasn't very busy in the evening. He had time between customers to work on his school assignments.

One afternoon a caseworker from the state Department of Labor came into the station. She asked the manager, Mr. Sawyer, whether Perry was old enough to be working in a gas station. He told her Perry had said he was 16.

The caseworker asked Perry whether he had a work permit. Perry said he didn't think he needed one. The caseworker said he must tell her how old he was. She was very serious. Perry knew he had to tell her his real age.

Child Labor Laws

The caseworker told the station manager he was in violation of the state's child labor law. She told Perry he would have to get a work permit. "Even with a permit," she said, "you will not be allowed to work in a gas station. The law prohibits young people under the age of 16 from working in gasoline stations and other places that are considered dangerous."

Compulsory Education and Child Labor: Two Laws that Work Together

Child labor laws were passed about 100 years ago. This was at the same time state governments passed their compulsory education laws. The two laws work hand in hand. The education laws make parents and schools see that every child is provided with an education. The child labor laws make parents and employers see that children work only when they are old enough and only under suitable conditions.

If you were working in violation of the child labor laws, you would not be penalized. Instead, your parents and the person employing you would be considered at fault.

The child labor laws also protect you from doing work that is dangerous. Perry cannot work in a gas station while he is under 16. The lawmakers in his state believed working in a gas station was dangerous for someone of that age.

Minors over age 12 (or 10 in some states) are allowed to do certain kinds of work. They can do yard work, baby-sit, have a newspaper route, and do certain types of non-hazardous farm work. But they can do these things only during nonschool hours. In most states, minors under 12 may not work outside the home. However, special laws allow children of any age to do stage and screen work.

Your Rights at Work

When you do work, you are protected by certain rights. You have the right to be paid for all the work you do. You have the right to be paid the *minimum wage* per hour. Minimum wages are set by Congress and by state legislatures.

You can find out what the minimum wage is in your state when you apply for a *work permit*. Usually work permits can be obtained at your school. If not, someone there should be able to tell you where you can get one.

Getting a work permit is important. You must have a permit to defend yourself if your rights are violated.

Work and School

Some young people believe that the education laws and child labor laws prevent them from exercising their rights. They want to be free to quit school and go to work. Your rights are restricted until you are 16 for your protection. The laws protect you now and when you are 16 and older.

"Hanging out" in most public places is usually okay, unless it violates laws against loitering or creating a nuisance.

Chapter 6

When You're Hanging Out

*J*erome *and Al were hanging out at a local coffee-house on Friday night. At around 10 PM, two police officers came up to them and told them that they had five minutes to finish their coffee and get home. If they didn't, they would be violating the town curfew. Al said he was allowed to be out because he was over eighteen. But Jerome was sixteen. As soon as the clock reached 10 PM, the police officers gave Jerome a ticket.*

The next day, Jerome called the police station and asked exactly what the law said. He was told that it was okay to be out after 10 PM if he was with some-one over eighteen and his parents knew where he was. In Jerome's case, both were true. He went to court to challenge the ticket, and the judge dismissed it.

Curfews on the Rise

Curfews are laws that prohibit people from being on the streets during certain hours. Although some curfews apply to adults, most apply to teens. Curfews are most often put in place to decrease juvenile crime late at night. While Jerome's circumstances allowed him to be out after 10 PM in his town, the rules about curfews vary from state to state. These days, more and more states are imposing curfews on teens. Cities as small as Charlottesville, Virginia, and as large as Los Angeles, California, are telling teens they have to be at home between the hours of 10 PM and 6 AM, unless accompanied by an adult.

If a teen violates the curfew, he or she may be given a ticket as Jerome was. Sometimes, a police officer will send the teen home with just a warning. Other times, a police officer will notify the teen's parents of the violation. If a teen is caught in a more serious act, he or she may be arrested and taken to the police station.

While you may not agree with curfews, the best thing to do if your town has one is to obey the law. To find out exactly what the law is, do what Jerome did. Call the police station and ask.

"Under Eighteen Not Admitted Without Parent or Guardian"

Almost everyone knows of a store that refuses to let kids under age 18, or 16, enter by themselves.

Usually it is the kind of store that sells things kids like. It may sell gum, comic books, candy bars, games, records, or tapes. If you have been kept out of a store, you may have asked yourself: "Don't I have a right to go into any store I want?"

The law does recognize a person's right to shop, but it is a right that can be restricted in some ways. Owners of stores can legally prevent young people from entering. What they cannot do is allow some young people to shop but not others.

A store that allowed white kids to shop but not black or Hispanic kids would be violating the *civil rights* laws. These are laws prohibiting different treatment of people because of race, sex, physical handicap, and some other reasons. We will hear more about civil rights in Chapter 11.

Shopping Malls: Public or Private?

Shopping malls raise more complicated questions about rights. A mall is actually a very large building. Inside the building are stores similar to the stores along a street. The owners of these stores can restrict who enters. There are also open areas inside the mall. These are known as *common areas*. Legally, common areas are like city streets and sidewalks. They belong to everyone. The mall owners cannot prevent anyone from entering the mall and using these common areas.

If you have visited malls with your friends, you may have had difficulty exercising your right to

walk or stand in these common areas. A mall security officer may have warned you that you will have
to leave the mall if you cause trouble. You may
have been told that it is illegal for more than three
or four of you to stand or walk around together.

Is it legal for malls to make their own rules and
force you to leave if you break a rule? Many law-
yers and judges would answer "No." When the mall
owners invite everyone to come into the mall, the
walkways become *public property.* This means the
mall owners must allow people to do all the things
they have a right to do on the streets and sidewalks
outside the mall.

Getting mall owners to agree not to make special
rules for young people is difficult. Can you do
anything about the rules at the mall you like to go
to? It will not be easy. It would help to have your
parents and your friends' parents request a meeting
with the mall owners, the mall security officers, and
the police chief and mayor or chief administrator of
your town.

Such a meeting could show the mall owners that
you and your friends are serious. It could show
that you understand that rights come with responsibilities, and that you take your responsibilities
seriously. The mall owners and security officers
might be surprised to find that young people know
so much about their rights.

Chapter 7

What About Sex and Pregnancy?

*C*amile and Terry have been dating for more than a year. They know a lot of their friends are having sex, but they haven't done it yet. Camile and Terry talk about it a lot, but they're both not sure they're ready. Also, they want to be careful. Neither one of them wants an unplanned pregnancy.

Camile thought about going on the pill. She didn't know whether she could get a prescription without having a parent's permission. Afraid to ask her family doctor, Camile went to a free family planning clinic. The nurse told her that because the clinic receives funds from the federal government, it must notify her parents before giving her a prescription. Camile didn't want to go behind her parents' back. She decided to talk to them first.

Your Sexual Rights

Your sexual rights are restricted until you are considered mature enough to exercise them freely. Young people mature at different ages, but states must set an official age for sexual maturity. This age is called the "age of consent." It is 18 in many states but younger in others. Until you reach this age, it is officially "against the law" for you to have sexual intercourse with anyone.

Age-of-consent laws are very old-fashioned. For example, most consent laws apply only to girls. There is no age of consent for boys. This is because the courts believe that young girls are more at risk than young boys. A young woman could become pregnant or have to have an abortion. As a result, the courts believe they have a legitimate concern for the well-being of young women.

The boy or man who violates the consent law is guilty of statutory rape. *Rape* occurs when a person is forced to have sex against her will. Statutory is a legal term. It means that a person is guilty of a crime because someone involved is younger than the age stated by law.

A boy or man is guilty of statutory rape if the girl with whom he has sexual intercourse is younger than the age of consent. He can be found guilty and punished *even if the girl consented to having intercourse.* Until she reaches the age of consent, the law restricts a girl's right to make her own decisions about sexual matters.

People over the age of 18 have the legal right to "consent" (agree) to sex with others over that age. Everyone—no matter what their age— has the legal right to refuse sex with anyone for any reason.

Your Rights if You Become Pregnant

When Sue's friend Amanda became pregnant, she went to a family planning center to get help. The counselor at the center suggested she have a blood test to be sure she was pregnant. Amanda told the counselor she didn't know what she would do if her father found out.

Amanda's test showed she was pregnant. She asked the counselor whether she could get an abortion. An abortion removes the developing egg from a woman's uterus. This ends her pregnancy.

The counselor explained that every woman has the right to end a pregnancy through an abortion. In some states, restrictions apply to young people. Some states require that girls obtain their parents' permission before having an abortion. Other states require that the girl's parents be told, but do not require the parents' permission.

Abortions and the Law

On Sunday evening, for no apparent reason, Amanda began to cry. When Amanda got control of herself, her mother asked her what was wrong. Amanda told her about getting pregnant, and her appointment for an abortion.

Amanda's mother was very glad Amanda had told her about what had happened. She told Amanda a very deep secret. When she was 17, she had an abortion too.

*"Abortions were completely illegal in those days,"
Amanda's mother said. "I had it done in a doctor's
office. It cost $300. My three girlfriends helped me
raise the money.*

*"The doctor's instruments weren't clean enough,
and I got an infection," Amanda's mother said. "My
temperature went up to 105° and I almost died.*

*"Since abortions were legalized," Amanda's
mother reassured her, "doctors can do them safely in
hospitals or clinics. The danger of something going
wrong is very small."*

The Right to Life and the Right to Choose

Up until about 20 years ago, it was illegal to have
an abortion in every state in the United States. The
Supreme Court gave their opinion about this. They
gave their answer in a very important case called
Roe vs. Wade.

The judges did not say that women have a right
to end a pregnancy through an abortion. What
they said was that ending a pregnancy is a *private*
decision.

The Supreme Court judges said that government and the law cannot interfere with people's
private decisions. Pregnant girls and women, along
with everyone else, have a *right to privacy.* One of
the things this right allows them to do is end a
pregnancy by having an abortion.

Women's right to privacy also allows them to prevent pregnancy by using birth control devices. These
rights are often called the right to choose or the right
of choice. They refer to a woman's right to decide
whether or not she wants to have a child.

Most people agree that there is such a thing as the
right to privacy. Many people do not agree that pregnancy and *abortion* are entirely private. They believe
that a baby comes to life at the moment a woman
becomes pregnant. They insist that this baby has a
right to life.

The supporters of the right to life want abortions
to be made illegal again. They claim that when an
abortion is performed a baby is being killed. They say
abortions must be made illegal to guarantee the right
of these babies to live.

Your Right to Keep Your Baby

Until a few years ago, a girl younger than the age of
consent who became pregnant and had her baby could
have the baby taken away by the legal system. But
things have changed. Today you have the right to
keep your baby in almost all cases.

Also, in the past, girls who became pregnant either
dropped out of school or were forced to leave. Today,
pregnant girls have a right to finish school, attend graduation, and participate in extracurricular activities.

Chapter 8

Drugs, Alcohol, and Your Rights

*L*iza and Sophie were hanging out in the school parking lot before the dance. Sophie had taken vodka from her parents' liquor cabinet, and she and Liza were mixing it with their sodas.

The girls were both psyched about the dance. Their crushes were supposed to be there, but they were nervous. They thought getting a buzz would help.

After a while, they decided to enter the school. As they approached the doors, they noticed a line forming. Sophie went up to see what was happening. Everyone was being forced to take a Breathalyzer test before being allowed into the dance. She walked back to where Liza was waiting and told her the scoop.

Liza and Sophie knew they couldn't go in, but they didn't want to miss the dance. They didn't want to drive home after drinking either. So instead they ended up hanging out in the parking lot all night.

Regulation of Alcohol

In most states, it is illegal to buy alcoholic beverages until you are 21. Until recently, some states had 18 as the *legal drinking age.* This is the same age at which young people can vote and exercise other adult rights. But with the rise of alcohol-related car accidents the age was raised to 21.

Your parents may allow you to drink at home under their supervision. Restrictions are necessary because alcohol, even in small amounts, can distort your judgment. Even for adults 21 and over, drinking is restricted. No one may drive a car if they have drunk more than a moderate amount.

Drugs: Legal and Illegal

Many drugs are regulated because they also can distort your judgment. They interfere with your ability to do ordinary tasks like driving a car.

Many drugs that doctors prescribe are dangerous. They can only be purchased at a drugstore with a prescription signed by a doctor.

You probably also know about illegal or "hard" drugs such as marijuana, cocaine, crack, and heroin. The laws against these drugs are very strict, partly because the drugs are distributed and sold by large networks of illegal suppliers and dealers that are difficult to control.

Drug traders are often involved in other illegal activities as well. Many of the people who buy and use the drugs get the money by illegal means.

Most states say you must be 21 years old to drink alcohol.

Searching for Drugs

Many schools force students to take Breathalyzer tests before going to a school dance or prom. Other schools force student athletes to take random drug tests, or search students' lockers for drugs.

Is this fair? The Bill of Rights protects you from illegal searches and seizures. This means the police can't search you or your property without probable cause. (A drug test is considered a search of a body.)

Without probable cause, schools in most states must get your consent. Contact your local chapter of the ACLU to learn about the privacy laws in schools of your state. They can also tell you how to take action if you think your privacy rights have been violated.

Drugs, Searches, and Parental Rights

When it comes to your parents, the laws about privacy, searches, and seizures do not apply. Your parents have the right to search your room, your clothes, or your book bag. They also can conduct a home drug test on you without your knowledge. You may think this is unfair. But parents often believe that they have no choice.

If you have questions about drugs, are being pressured to take them, or think you have a problem with them, talk with your parents. Hopefully, you and your parents can communicate openly and come up with a solution together.

Chapter 9

Gerald and the Juvenile Justice System

*G*erald and his friend Ronnie called Mrs. Cook on the telephone and said some "dirty" words to her. Mrs. Cook called the police. The police were able to find out that the call came from Gerald's house. They went there and found Gerald and Ronnie. They took them to a juvenile detention center. A juvenile detention center is a place where young people are kept when they are arrested by the police.

The next day a juvenile court judge had a hearing about Gerald. Juvenile courts handle cases involving young people. They are a separate system from the courts and judges for adults. The judge asked Gerald questions. Mrs. Cook was not there.

A few days later there was a second hearing. The judge decided that Gerald must go to the state industrial training school. He would have to stay there until he reached his majority.

An industrial training school is not a regular school. It is actually a type of jail for young people. Majority is the age at which a person legally becomes an adult. In most states an 18-year-old is considered an adult. Gerald was 15.

Gerald's parents spent three years going to other courts trying to get Gerald free. Finally, the Supreme Court decided that Gerald's parents were right. By that time, Gerald had become 18.

If you believe any of your legal rights have been violated, you can seek the advice of a lawyer.

Gerald and the Supreme Court

What happened to Gerald is a true story. Gerald's full name is Gerald Gault.

The Supreme Court said that Gerald was prevented from exercising his rights. A person who is arrested has several rights.

• The right to be considered innocent until proved otherwise.

• The right to be represented by a lawyer.

• If the arrested person cannot pay a lawyer, the government must provide one.

• The right to refuse to answer any questions that may *incriminate*—make the person seem guilty.

• The right to see the people who say you broke the law and to ask them any questions.

Since Gerald won his case, things have changed a great deal. If you are arrested today and brought before a judge, you have the right to be represented by a lawyer. The police and the judge must prove that you did the things you are accused of doing. They must let your lawyer try to prove that you did *not* do what the police claim you did.

You can *appeal* the decision of the judge. In an appeal, you ask a second judge to determine whether mistakes were made at your trial and whether your rights were restricted or denied.

The law provides citizens with many rights if they are arrested or
taken into custody.

Chapter 10

The Juvenile Justice System and You

There are two ways in which you can become involved with the juvenile justice system. The first is to be *taken into custody* for breaking the law. Being taken into custody means that a police officer or court officer takes you to a juvenile detention center. There they indicate what crime you have been accused of.

Being taken into custody is like being arrested. The difference is that you can be taken without proof if a police officer or court officer *thinks* you have done something wrong.

In many cases, if the young people who were taken into custody had been treated the way adults are treated, they could not have been arrested. Why not? Because there was not enough evidence to prove they had committed crimes.

You can also be brought into the juvenile justice system if you cannot control how you act and your parents are no longer able to help you control yourself. In some states you would be referred to as a *Person In Need of Supervision* (PINS for short).

The most common reasons young people are considered in need of supervision are (1) being repeatedly absent from school, (2) running away from home, and (3) constantly fighting with their parents. You do not have to break a specific law or commit a crime to become a PINS.

How the Juvenile Justice System May Treat You

If you are taken into the system, you have the right to *due process*. Due process is a legal term meaning that all of your rights must be respected. These include your right to be represented by a lawyer and your right to know the exact reasons why you have been brought in. These rights are discussed in Chapter 9.

If a judge decides something must be done about you, there are three kinds of action she or he can order. The first is *probation*. Probation is a legal term meaning that you will be supervised by an officer of the court for a specific period of time. The officers are called *probation officers*. The period of time might be as short as six months or as long as two or three years.

If you are on probation you must meet regularly with a probation officer. Usually you will agree to certain things that the officer thinks are necessary.

The second type of action the judge might order is that you attend a special school. Sometimes these are called industrial training schools, the type Gerald Gault was sent to in Arizona. Sometimes they are called *reform schools*. These schools are basically prisons, but they do provide courses like ordinary schools. The doors are locked, however, and the outdoor areas are fenced in.

Being Tried as an Adult

The third type of action the judge can order is that you be tried as an adult. When this happens, your case is transferred to a regular judge of the criminal court system. You may have a trial, or you may arrange a *plea bargain*. In a plea bargain, the person charged with committing a crime agrees to admit being guilty. The judge responds by ordering a less severe punishment.

The number of young people tried as adults has been increasing steadily. Most of these young people have committed very serious crimes. For example, if a young person kills someone with a gun, he or she will probably be tried as an adult. A young person who is heavily involved in drug dealing can also be tried by the courts as an adult.

If someone is tried as a juvenile, the judge cannot order a sentence that continues beyond age 21.

Rosa Parks helped to spark the civil rights movement of the 1960s. In Alabama in 1955, she refused to give up her seat on a bus to a white person.

Chapter 11

Protecting Your Rights

January 15 is the day Americans honor Dr. Martin Luther King, Jr. for his accomplishments as a leader of the *civil rights movement* in the United States. The civil rights movement was a struggle to make sure that all people can fully exercise their rights. Age, sex, race, or religion cannot be the reason for treating any one person differently from another.

The struggle for American civil rights began in colonial times. On July 4, Americans celebrate the adoption of the Declaration of Independence in 1776. The Declaration was another important part of the struggle for our rights. On Presidents' Day, in February, Americans honor George Washington and Abraham Lincoln. As the first president of the United States, Washington helped make sure that the Bill of Rights was added to the Constitution.

Abraham Lincoln was president of the United States during the Civil War. We remember him for helping to eliminate slavery. After the Civil War, important amendments were added to the Constitution. These amendments made slavery illegal, gave former slaves the right to vote, and guaranteed all U.S. citizens equal protection under the law.

Fighting for Your Rights

Even though many people have fought for your basic rights in the past, that doesn't mean there's nothing left to fight for. You must continue to fight to preserve your rights. And the best way to do that is to learn what those rights are. You may already feel as if politicians, teachers, and parents are trying to take more and more control away from you. There are times when this may be necessary to keep you safe. But there may also be times when your rights are violated, and it's often up to you to take a stand. That's what Charlie Gustin of Farwell, Texas, did.

When Charlie was seventeen years old, his high school adopted a new policy. It stated that anyone who wanted to participate in extracurricular activities had to agree to random drug tests. Charlie thought this was totally unfair. He was an honors student. He had just gotten a full scholarship to college. But most important, Charlie had just finished taking a class on government and the U.S. Constitution.

Charlie believed that this policy was unconstitutional. He refused to allow the drug test. As a result, the

After being shot in an assassination attempt in 1981, James Brady worked to strengthen laws against guns. In 1991, a gun-control measure—known as the Brady Bill— was finally approved by Congress.

school forbade him to participate in any after-school activities. Charlie decided to sue the school district. He stated that the test was an illegal search and violated his right against illegal search and seizure.

With the help of the ACLU, Charlie was allowed to continue with his extracurricular activities until graduation. Once he went off to college, he dropped the lawsuit. But along the way, Charlie learned what it means to take a stand and fight the system.

What Can I Do?

Here are some tips to help you safely protect your civil rights at school:

- Don't take anything illegal to school. Yes, you have the right to privacy, but the 4th Amendment does not protect you if you carry drugs or weapons to school.
- If the principal wants to search your locker, you don't have to say yes. You can object, but do so politely.
- If you're upset about a search or a new school policy, don't get involved in a physical confrontation. It's always best to stay calm and protest verbally, not physically. Remember, responsibilities come with rights. If you want your rights respected, you must respect the rights of others.
- Don't be afraid to voice your opinion. If your school newspaper has an opinion column, write a piece about something that upsets you. Or start a civil rights club at school. There is strength in numbers.

If you think you have a case against your school, contact the ACLU, then talk to your parents and decide whether it's worth the fight.

Glossary

abortion   A procedure that removes a developing ovum or "egg," ending a pregnancy.

abuse   Treating someone in a way that is cruel and harmful.

age of consent   Age at which young people may marry without parental permission; also age at which a young woman may legally agree to have sexual intercourse.

appeal   A procedure that allows a young person to take the decision of a juvenile court judge to another, higher court.

Bill of Rights   The proclamation of your most important rights and freedoms in the first ten amendments to the Constitution.

civil rights   The personal rights and freedoms of individuals.

custody   An official decision, by a judge, about who will be responsible for taking care of a child or a young person.

divorce   The legal ending of a marriage.

freedom of speech   Your right to say what you wish whenever and wherever you desire.

freedom of the press   Your right to print whatever you wish in a book, pamphlet, newspaper, or magazine.

industrial training school   A special school that supervises young people who have committed serious crimes.

juvenile court   A system of judges and officers who listen to complaints against young people.

juvenile detention center   Where young people are kept before they see a juvenile court judge.

lawyer   A person who legally practices law.

minimum wage   The lowest amount of money per hour that may be paid legally to a worker.

neglect   A failure to do the things one is required to do for another person.

nuisance   A thing or activity that interferes with someone's enjoyment, causes them physical discomfort, or makes them afraid they will be injured.

PINS   Person In Need of Supervision; a young person who cannot be controlled by his or her parents or teachers.

rape   Forcing a woman to have sexual intercourse against her will.

reform school   A school that supervises young people who have committed serious crimes.

rehabilitation   Enabling people to learn to control their behavior.

rights   Your basic freedom.

separation   A legal agreement between husband and wife to live apart.

Supreme Court   The highest court in the American legal system, made up of nine judges appointed by the President.

work permit   A document that allows a young person to work at a particular job.

Where to Go for Help

If talking to your parents is a problem, go to teachers you trust, your friends' parents, your school librarian, school nurse, or a minister, rabbi, or YWCA or YMCA leader you know and trust.

You can also find help at local and state agencies including the Public Defender's Office, Legal Aid Society, Legal Assistance Association, and the state chapter or affiliate of the American Civil Liberties Union.

National Organizations:

American Civil Liberties Union (ACLU)
125 Broad Street
18th Floor
New York, NY 10004
(212) 549-2500

NAACP Legal Defense Fund
99 Hudson Street
New York, NY 10013
(800) 221-7822
(212) 219-1900

Children's Defense Fund Legal Division
25 E Street, NW
Washington, DC 20001
(202) 628-8787
Web site: http://www.childrensdefense.org

Youth Law Center
114 Sansome Street
Suite 950
San Francisco, CA 94104
(415) 543-3379

Hotlines:

Child Abuse Prevention Information Resources Center
(800) 342-7472

Office of Children and Family Services
(800) 345-5437

Youth Crisis Hotline
(800) 448-4663

For Further Reading

Evans, J. Edward. *Freedom of Speech*. Minneapolis, MN: Lerner Publications, 1990.

Gora, Joel M., et al. *The Right to Protest: The Basic ACLU Guide to Free Expression*. Carbondale, IL: Southern Illinois University Press, 1991.

Greenberg, Keith Elliot, and Jeanne Vestal, eds. *Adolescent Rights: Are Young People Equal Under the Law?* New York: Twenty-First Century Books, 1995.

Hempleman, Kathleen A. *Teen Legal Rights: A Guide for the '90s*. Westport, CT: Greenwood Press, 1994.

Jacobs, Thomas A. *What Are My Rights? 95 Questions and Answers About Teens and the Law*. Minneapolis, MN: Free Spirit, 1997.

Landau, Elaine. *Your Legal Rights: From Custody Battles to School Searches, The Headline-Making Cases That Affect Your Life*. New York: Walker and Company, 1995.

Meltzer, Milton. *The Bill of Rights: How We Got It and What It Means*. New York: Thomas Y. Crowell, 1992.

Index

About the Author

Kenneth Fox is an author and a university professor. He was codirector of the Washington Mini-School in Washington, DC, an experimental program for sixth-graders about government, the law, young people's rights, and making places for children in adult organizations. He has written on the law and American cities and on the history of American cities. He has taught history and public administration at the University of Massachusetts, Yale University, and Rutgers University.

Acknowledgments and Photo Credits

Cover photo by Chuck Peterson.
All other photographs by Stuart Rabinowitz, except page 2, Chris Volpe;
page 50, © Jean Marc Giboux/Gamma Liaison; pages 54, 57, Wide World
Photos.